BANKRUPTCY DIDN'T *BREAK* ME!

Learn the Keys to Success

BANKRUPTCY DIDN'T *BREAK* ME!

© Copyright 2006, 2017, 2020 by Kassondra R Lewis

All rights reserved. This book is protected by the copyright laws of the United States of America. No portion of this book stored electronically, transmitted, reproduced or reprinted for commercial gain or profit without prior written permission from Just-4-U Publishing, a Division of KGSL Enterprises & KGSL LLC.

www.askkassondratv.com

Telephone: 1-800-645-8220

Third Edition: January 2020

Cover and design by Stefanie Fontecha with Beetiful Book Covers
Review and editing assistance by Christina Williams and Josette Mills
Proofreading done by Jen FitzGerald with C.P. Proofreading & More
ISBN 978-0-9986769-1-3

Printed in the U.S.A

BANKRUPTCY DIDN'T *BREAK* ME!

Learn the Keys to Success

KASSONDRA R. LEWIS

DEDICATION

I dedicate this book to my mother, Lois J. Sylva Lewis, who taught me to never give up on my dreams. Life can be challenging, but I will make it through with God on my side.

I also dedicate this book to every person who pursues the American Dream of Home Ownership.

SPECIAL THANKS:

To all my family and friends for their unwavering love and support. Especially my uncle, Tyronne J. Sylva; my sister, Myrtle Sonora Lewis Mosby; my brother, Gene E. Lewis Jr.; and my sister-in-law, Kimberly Lewis.

To Lisa Nichols for helping me get past my pain and showing me how to share my story to be a blessing to others.

To Susie Carder for teaching me how to get out of my own way and pushing me into my destiny.

To Kathy Kidd for listening and sharing her knowledge to help make be a better author.

Table of Contents

Chapter 1	Why am I Here?	1
Chapter 2	The Journey	2
Chapter 3	Changing my Attitude and Mindset	5
Chapter 4	Defining Success for Yourself	7
Chapter 5	What is Bankruptcy?	8
Chapter 6	What are the differences between Bankruptcies?	9
Chapter 7	Fact and Fiction about Bankruptcy	10
Chapter 8	What is my Plan?	12
Chapter 9	Mortgage Insider Tips	15
Chapter 10	Understanding your Credit Report and Financial Character	19
Chapter 11	What is Debt-To-Income Ratio (DTI) and how does it affect me?	22
Chapter 12	How to clean up your credit report for Free	25
Chapter 13	Celebrating Milestones and Achieving Success	27

Chapter 1
Why am I Here?

I'm here as a result of my learned ability to recover quickly from a job loss, foreclosure and bankruptcy. I now live in my dream home with a low interest rate of 3.625% and my automobile has a low rate of .9%. I have rebuilt my credit to a 700 score and I enjoy the benefits of traveling when I want to, having a savings account and building my home-based business. I can help you achieve these same results.

This journey has been tough, but, in the end, I've come out stronger and more financially stable. I'd like to share my knowledge, experiences, lessons and tips with you in hopes that I can help you save time on your recovery journey and set you up for success.

Hi, my name is Kassondra R. Lewis and I am your Mortgage Insider and Coach.

My perspective is unique because it is twofold. Not only have I personally experienced the hardships of life events and recovered, but I have also worked in the mortgage industry for over 16 years in various positions.

I'm a mortgage underwriter and a processing manager. An underwriter is the person who approves home loans with conditions to be met. The processing manager is the one who manages a team of processors and the loan pipeline to ensure loans close on time. The public doesn't have access to the underwriter and I'm going to change that by pulling back the curtains and sharing some information with you.

If anyone can tell you how to overcome certain life events, rebuild your credit and qualify for a new home loan with low interest rates, I can.

Chapter 2

The Journey

Let's be honest, shall we? The truth about bankruptcy is that it brings a whole string of emotions and, if we aren't careful, we can get stuck on the emotional rollercoaster.

No one wants to talk about the taboo subject of bankruptcy and foreclosure. Mainly because you don't want to be judged and criticized. You're already hurt, embarrassed, scared and feel like a failure for being unable to control the situation. You don't want your friends and family to know what you're dealing with, and that puts you in a dangerous position of isolation.

You might be surprised at how many of them have already been through bankruptcy, but you're paralyzed and too embarrassed to ask questions or ask for help, so you lose a lot of time and resources.

Today I can see clearly what my path to success requires, however, this wasn't always the case. Have you ever felt hopeless and helpless? Have you ever been so overwhelmed you don't know which way to go? Have you ever been afraid to simply answer the phone because a creditor or collection agency might be on the other end? Have you ever had to stand in line for assistance in paying your utility bill or for food stamps? I know both of these experiences and then some far too well.

I've gone through bankruptcy not once, but three times due to job loss, divorce and then a secondary job loss when the national mortgage crisis struck.

This last time really took me to my emotional edge.

Although I had gone through this before and knew how to execute a plan, I was more scared and stuck than ever before. You see, this

Chapter 2

time my life wasn't the only one affected by my financial devastation. I knew that I would have to tell three families they were going to be displaced; leaving "home" as they knew it.

At the time of the last bankruptcy, I owned four homes with three of the homes being rental properties. I was an ethical landlord; investing in my community by renting to those who had challenging credit issues, were not in a position to purchase, yet needed affordable housing.

The plan was to give my tenants an opportunity to get on their feet with the hopes of them purchasing the home they were renting.

All those hopes went out the window when the mortgage crisis hit home. Never in my wildest dreams did I ever THINK the real estate market could collapse to the point of putting mortgage companies, banks and historically established lenders out of business.

I remember it like it was yesterday. My mind raced as I drove home from downtown after another failed attempt to get the money to pay my mortgage. My phone was ringing and I was scared to answer it. My heart was beating so fast I could hear it over the radio. It became harder to drive as the tears ran down my face uncontrollably. As I was thinking "God what am I going to do now?" the realization that I was about to lose it all hit me like a ton of bricks.

The phone rang again but that time I answered it. It was my sister calling to check on me and I couldn't talk. All I could say was "I have to call you back" and hung up the phone. The stress and tears were too much and I had to pull off the interstate into the parking lot of a company that had gone out of business. I got out of the car yelling and screaming, crying and praying. I couldn't hold it together anymore. I don't know how long I was out there with my car still running, but I heard a song on the radio saying "Shake the devil off," by Dorothy Norwood. I remember yelling "Why me, God? I didn't do anything wrong. I was helping people. How am I going to tell them they have to find somewhere else to live? This isn't their fault but I can't stop this from happening. I don't want to go through this."

Chapter 2

Somehow, I was finally able to get back in my car and continue to drive home. The tears were still coming and I couldn't stop the thoughts that were all over the place. As I pulled into my garage and closed the door, my phone rang again. It was my sister again, but this time she had my brother on the phone too. She said she'd heard something in my voice and wanted me to tell them what was wrong so they could help.

I started crying even more and sharing everything I was dealing with; how I was about to lose everything I'd worked so hard to rebuild. I told them there wasn't anything anyone could do. I was out of a job and even if I filed bankruptcy that wasn't going to help protect the three families. I was still sitting in the car crying and yelling when my boyfriend opened the house door leading to the garage to check on me; his face showed helplessness as he dropped his head and closed the door.

Have you ever felt like giving up? I don't know how long we were on the phone, but I finally turned off the car, hung up the phone and went into the house. I didn't get much sleep that night, but a new day brought a new perspective.

I share this with you because that was one of the hardest and lowest points of my life. The lesson I learned was that no matter what you are going through, if you are blessed (or fortunate) enough to have the love and support of your family, you must decide to let them in. Even when we feel most alone, there is support all around us.

I wrote this book because I realized that in speaking my truth in sharing my pain and vulnerability that someone else might find their own strength. This is why I am here!

I've learned some lessons that I must share to help others. Bankruptcy Didn't Break Me! I am here to make sure it doesn't BREAK you!

I have been where you are and I know the way out.

Chapter 3

Changing my Attitude and Mindset

I survived my emotions and got a handle on them, so then I had to check my attitude. I accepted that there was nothing I could do to change what was about to happen, so I had to learn all I could to set myself up to be successful after bankruptcy was over.

Attitude and perspective is key. We can't think of ourselves as victims, otherwise we'll never make it past the emotional rollercoaster. We must acknowledge the situation and our part in it, no matter how big or small.

I started talking to myself and giving myself pep talks. I said, "Ok, self, there must be another lesson God wants me to learn." Why? I know that when you don't learn the lessons of the past, you are bound to repeat them. I had to take responsibility for my part and acknowledge that I missed something the first two times; I was going through bankruptcy a third time.

I acknowledged that I had a consumer mindset and was spending every penny I made. I didn't want to live on a budget, so I didn't follow it consistently. I just put some money in the bank and left it there rather than having the savings habit of putting money away every time I got paid. So, for me, those were the lessons I missed.

I took on the attitude that I'm a **SURVIVOR** and nothing and no one was going to stop me from achieving my goals. I might have been delayed, but I still accomplished my goals and dreams.

I dusted myself off, wiped away my tears and got back into the game. The game of life. Life is a journey and it's all about the lessons we learn along the way that help build our character and make us stronger.

It's about the relationships we form. How we help and nurture each other. We're stronger than we think.

My attitude and mindset are now what keeps me aligned with my plan. My credit is good again. I bought a new home. I'm a producer, not a consumer. I'm a saver, not a spender. I live on a budget, so I can be a good steward and direct my money where to go. I was already a tither, so that didn't change. I learned that there is more to good stewardship than just being a tither.

Chapter 4

Defining Success for Yourself

How do you define success? This is a very important question, because you've got to know for yourself what's important to you. Is it family and friends, your job, your income or your status or position in life? To be successful, **YOU MUST BE PREPARED FOR THE SUCCESS YOU ARE PURSUING!**

There are many successful entrepreneurs who have given opinions about what is truly important in life. I say, whatever your beliefs, just stay true to yourself.

I personally hold dear my adopted definition of success that may be the same as what you believe to be true for your own life.

I define success as: *"When preparation meets opportunity."* It's short, sweet and very, very true. The fact is:

- To be hired for a job, you must be prepared and show up for the interview to be offered an opportunity.
- To get any good deal, you must be prepared financially to pay for it and show up at the assigned time.
- To purchase a home, you must prepare your credit and finances so that when you find your dream home, the opportunity doesn't pass you by because you failed to be prepared for it.

Success for me means owning my own home and the car that I desire. Having a savings account and not living paycheck-to-paycheck. Being able to travel at will and knowing it's in my budget. Being able to be there and support family when they need it. I will be successful and bankruptcy will NOT stand in my way. Now I must ***UNDERSTAND*** bankruptcy.

Chapter 5
What is Bankruptcy?

The simple truth in plain English: **Bankruptcy is a process that allows consumers and businesses to repay none, some or all of their debts under the protection of the federal bankruptcy court.** Depending on which bankruptcy you qualify for it is possible to discharge all your debt under Chapter 7 or file a repayment plan under Chapter 13. For the benefits of this book we will only cover personal bankruptcies Chapter 7 & 13; not business bankruptcy known as Chapter 11.

Bankruptcy is also the only legal action that will stop a foreclosure, repossession or garnishment being pursued against you if filed in a timely manner.

Chapter 6
What are the differences between Bankruptcies?

There are two different types of personal bankruptcies that you can file for and they're known as Chapter 7 and Chapter 13. The other two are known as Chapter 11 for businesses and Chapter 12 for farmers that we won't go into detail about in this book.

Chapter 7 – This is a full discharge or elimination of all debt to all creditors with the exception of any debt that you "reaffirm" with a creditor and/or is not dischargeable under federal law (i.e. student loans, state and federal tax liens, etc.). There are exemptions under the law that require you to give up property which exceeds certain limits so that it can be sold to pay off creditors.

Chapter 13 – This is used when you don't qualify for a Chapter 7 because you make enough income to repay your creditors over a period of 3-5 years. This allows you to put all your creditors on a budget. The budget is approved and managed by the trustee of the court. You agree that a certain amount of your income is paid to the court trustee and the court in turn pays a certain amount to each creditor until all the debt is paid.

If you need further information, please contact a bankruptcy attorney to discuss the particulars of your case.

Chapter 7

Fact and Fiction about Bankruptcy

Fact 1: Bankruptcy is a law designed to help each citizen and business organization or entity with a legitimate way to relieve them of overwhelming debt that can no longer be managed by their best efforts and current finances.

Fiction: Bankruptcy is an action to be taken on a whim because you choose to spend frivolously and don't want to honor your responsibilities. This is what you see when one person's credit report shows numerous bankruptcy filings and their payment history still reflects ongoing late payments and collections even after bankruptcy.

Fact 2: Bankruptcy is a legal recourse to prevent foreclosures, repossessions and garnishments.

Fiction: Bankruptcy is to be used to buy time with a creditor by filing bankruptcy and dismissing it at a later date only to file again. Be honest. You can either work it out with your creditor or you need protection but you can't have both.

Fact 3: Bankruptcy stays on your credit report for ten years, but some creditors may choose to remove it after seven years. Doesn't usually happen but it's possible.

Fiction: You have to wait until bankruptcy is off your credit to start pursuing new credit. This isn't true and if you get in the habit of paying everything in cash, you're only hurting yourself.

Living debt-free is wonderful; however, you must remember that the only record a creditor or lender has of your financial character is your credit report. If you haven't re-established credit, then you have no new paper trail to prove that you've been more financially responsible since bankruptcy, so don't expect that your credit score has changed.

Fact 4: Always start new credit immediately after discharge to rebuild and re-establish good payment history.

Fact 5: Is it possible to buy a new home while in Chapter 13? Yes. The most lenient loan will be the FHA loan. This is a government loan, but it does require permission from the trustee of the bankruptcy court and proof of a 12-month payment history showing the court was paid on time. The lender may also ask for a signed letter of explanation of how you're budgeting to pay for the home, especially if the payment is higher than your current rent amount.

Fiction: Government loans aren't possible or are hard to get after bankruptcy. The truth is that government loans such as FHA are more forgiving and easier to get than a conventional loan.

Fact 6: Bankruptcy is not your friend. It is a last resort to keep your sanity and a stable lifestyle.

Fact 7: Bankruptcy will stop you from getting lower interest rates on credit cards or department store cards for a few years based on the rules of the company. It is true that bankruptcy lowers your credit score, which is what causes you to have higher rates. However, the more you re-establish your credit and improve your score, with more time after your bankruptcy, the rates will get better.

Once I had more information about bankruptcy, I was able to develop a plan so that I could be successful and rebound more quickly after bankruptcy.

Chapter 8

What is my Plan?

To understand how to best make a plan we must first understand our goals. All goals should be attainable which means ***measurable progress in reasonable time.***

What is a goal/objective: It is a desired result or possible outcome that a person or a system envisions, plans and commits to achieve.

What is a plan: It is a list of steps with timing and resources, used to achieve an objective.

Now that we understand that a plan is an outline of the steps to accomplish our goals, we first need to decide on our goals.

Here is an example of the goals I set:

- I wanted it ALL back within three years.
- Good credit means a credit score between 650-720. I wasn't satisfied with just having a 620. I had a 686 score prior to bankruptcy; new goal was to exceed that score.
- A new job.
- A new home.
- A new car.
- A savings account with $5000 minimum.

Now I needed to put them into a plan with timelines that were attainable.

My plan:

- I received the bankruptcy discharge letter.

Chapter 8

- Pulled my credit report to ensure accuracy showing the discharge date and all accounts.
- Immediately applied for two new unsecured credit cards so that I would have 12 months of history on two accounts at the end of year one after bankruptcy.
- Kept looking for a better job with higher pay.
- Beginning of year two I pulled my credit again to review how much my score had increased.
- Opened another new account as an unsecured small line of credit of $500. This gave my credit variety.
- At the end of 24 months after bankruptcy, I had three re-established accounts. Two with a 24-month history and one with a 12-month history.
- If all I'd had was a bankruptcy, I would have been in position to apply for a new home loan mortgage. But since I also had a foreclosure, the wait period on an FHA loan was three years from the discharge date. I had one more year to prepare.
- I found a new job and was able to start saving money. I saved $50 per paycheck with a goal of $1300 at the end of year three after bankruptcy.
- Three years after the bankruptcy was discharged, I had two accounts with a great 36-month history, one account with a 24-month history and my FICO score was back over 670. I had $1300 saved and I could plan on my tax refund to add to it for a down payment.
- I was then in position to buy a new home with a low interest rate. FHA loans will give you the same low interest rate regardless of credit score. Which means you get the same low rate as someone who has a credit score of 700.
- Always buy a home before buying a new automobile. Why? Because you have to monitor your debt-to-income ratio and you can buy an automobile anytime because they are more lenient with debt-to-income ratios. If you buy a new car first, you might limit how much of a home you can buy because of your debt-to-income ratios.

My attitude was accepting the fact that my life had taken a 3-year detour, but I was back on track to getting everything I wanted and what represents success to me.

My plan gave me the courage to move forward and I was able see a way out. My emotion changed to **relief**. No more creditor calls and no more stress. Starting life over was no longer such a bad thing. My thoughts were positive and it was easier to counteract any negative thoughts or doubts. I stayed focused on my plan.

I also began living my life based on the ***ANT Philosophy***. Which is, simply put, keep working and if something blocks or hinders the way, find another way to go around it, go over it or go through it, but always reach your goals. **Ants never quit.**

Chapter 9
Mortgage Insider Tips

Once I knew what goals I wanted to accomplish and I mapped out a timeline for my plan. I did some research and gained knowledge of what it took to ensure my mortgage loan got approved and what the best companies were to help rebuild my credit. I needed to make sure I was well informed so that my plan would work. I armed myself with knowledge.

TIP: Did you know that each type of mortgage has specific wait periods for derogatory life events like bankruptcy and foreclosure? See basic standards below

FHA and USDA (rural) Loans are government loans and they are more forgiving and/or lenient toward borrowers that have experienced life events.

- **Bankruptcy Chapter 7 has a 24-month wait period from the discharge date** or a 48-month period from the dismissal date. The concern is whether the bankruptcy was caused by a life event out of your control or if it was due to financial mismanagement.
- **Foreclosure has a 36-month wait period from the discharge date**. If you have had both bankruptcy and foreclosure you must meet both wait periods.
- **A Short Sale/Deed In Lieu Of is treated like a foreclosure and has a 36-month wait period from the discharge date.**
- **Bankruptcy Chapter 13 usually only requires 1 day after discharge**. However, some lenders may have what's called an overlay and still require that you have twelve months of re-established credit after the discharge. FHA prefers a 24 month

Chapter 9

wait but will allow less on a manual underwrite with stricter guidelines.

- **Extenuating circumstances** are allowed but very hard to document so most lenders won't allow them.

Conventional loans:

- **Bankruptcy has a 48-month wait period from the discharge date.**

- **A Short Sale/Deed In Lieu Of has a 48-month wait period.**

- **Foreclosure has a 7-year wait period from the discharge date.**

Note: If you had bankruptcy and foreclosure and the property was not reaffirmed (retained) in the bankruptcy and it was given back to the lender (surrendered), then it is possible to only have to wait the 48-month wait period since the foreclosure was part of the bankruptcy, but it depends on the lender/mortgage company.

Best card I found to rebuild credit:

I can tell you from experience that one of the best companies to use to rebuild your credit is **Capital One**. They are willing to give consumers a second chance as soon as 1 day after the bankruptcy discharge date. However, be mindful that the interest rates will be high, but that isn't your focus right now. Your goal is to open two new accounts immediately so that you can improve your credit score. Once time has passed and your credit score is higher, you can request a lower interest rate. You must prove you are credit worthy again.

Capital One will also allow you open more than one account. I believe their limit is three accounts. This also includes any type of business credit card. If you have a home-based business, they are more willing after bankruptcy to give you a second chance.

Chapter 9

Line of credit:

Apply for an unsecured line of credit. Go to your local bank or credit union that you do business with on a daily basis and request to open a line of credit. Let them know you're working to rebuild your credit and they will usually work with you. If they require it to be secured with a deposit, you really don't want this type of account unless you have no other choice. I would suggest going to another bank first and if you can't get an unsecured line of credit for $250 or $500 then you can do one secured account.

Secured accounts don't really help you much because they are guaranteed with a deposit. Creditors want to see that you are managing the credit limit you were granted and making payments on time.

TIP: Lines of credit are always good because you can treat them as an emergency account. Once it is paid off, the line stays available to you until you close the account. So if an emergency arises, you can use this line before using your cash savings.

Credit scores increase better when you have a variety of different types of credit extended to you. Like installment debts such as a mortgage, auto loan, student loan along with a line of credit, revolving credit cards, etc.

Note: Paying on time means on or before the due date. Most credit cards don't have grace periods and if you miss your due date, they will apply a late fee even though it's not reported on your credit. The reason it's not reported is because only payments that are more than thirty days late are reported on the credit report.

However, when you request reducing your interest rate and your payment history shows several late fees, they probably won't reduce your rate because you're not exactly paying on time.

Remember, this is a new start to get it right, so change your habits and make sure all debts, including utilities, are paid on time. It's a very

Chapter 9

good habit to avoid wasting money on late fees. If you don't believe me, then add up all the late fees you've paid on all your accounts in the last twelve months and you'll see how much money you lost or, should I say, gave away. It could have gone to your savings account instead.

Chapter 10

Understanding your Credit Report and Financial Character

A credit report represents your financial character. It tells every creditor and/or lender how you make your payments.

Based on how you make your payments, whether timely or late or via collections, a creditor will determine whether to extend you more credit. They are assessing how much of a risk you are based on your history.

It's important to understand that it's not just whether you have the ability to pay back a loan, it's whether you have the willingness to pay back the loan.

If you treat your accounts as insignificant and chose when to pay them rather than paying on time as you agreed when you requested the credit, then you're telling the creditor that your financial character is not strong. They can't trust what you say because your payment history shows that you don't care to honor your debts.

A $25 monthly payment may not seem like a lot or that it matters. However, if you choose to pay it late, meaning over thirty days late, and it's notated on your credit, it basically says you can't handle the current debt that you have. So why would a lender want to risk approving you for more credit?

There are three main credit bureaus that report your payment history: Equifax, Transunion and Experian. The credit scores, also known as a FICO score, range from 300-950. The average score is in the middle 600s and that's okay, but when you want lower rates on a loan or credit card, you really need to be at a score of 680 or higher. The higher the score, the lower the interest rate.

Your credit report will show your name, any alternative names, address, date of birth and social security number. It will report how many months each account has been reviewed and how many payments were paid as agreed, as well as any derogatory or late creditor accounts showing 30, 60, 90 and 120-day late payments. It will report public records like any state or federal tax liens, judgments, and bankruptcies. It will show your previous address and inquiries in the last ninety days to two years.

When a mortgage lender looks at your credit report, they first look at your credit score/FICO to determine if you meet the guidelines they have for the loan program you have applied for. They then verify that the information on the credit report reflects the information you gave them on the application and, if there are discrepancies, they will request additional documentation from you to clarify.

They will review carefully how well you have paid your current accounts and whether your history shows you have a willingness to pay your creditors. They will determine whether your collections or public records old or new have an effect on your loan approval.

What can you do to maximize the best score possible?

Before you start house hunting, please check out how you look on paper. Get a copy of your credit report and make sure all of the items are correct. If they are not then request corrections. Once you have had your credit report properly corrected take the next step by following these tips and your credit score will go up instantly.

Tip 1: You get more points from a revolving account, so if you have credit cards with balances, take a look at your limit compared to your balance. If your account is maxed to the limit, then either pay it down to $0 to totally maximize your points or pay it down to 30% or less of the high credit limit. Doing this shows that you are responsible enough to procure credit and not max it out and keep it there, thus increasing your score. Make sure your payments have posted to your account and it's updated to reflect the higher score before applying for a mortgage or any other loan.

However, I would suggest you only pay it down to a $10 balance. You get more points when the algorithm reads a small balance verses a $0 balance.

Tip 2: Don't close an account just because you're not using it. This is a common mistake that hurts you, because the moment the account is closed you lose credit for the long history that you had the account open. Simply keep it at a zero balance. This shows that you know how to manage the credit given to you. Don't forget the longer length of time your account is open, the more points it accumulates. However, be sure the total credit extended to you is not excessive.

Tip 3: When at all possible, you should consolidate your student loans into one account with a lower payment and not several small accounts. It always looks better to have fewer creditors to help minimize payments.

Tip 4: You want to avoid collections at all cost. They have such a negative effect on your credit score and your financial character. They drop your score quickly every time you get a collection.

How do you avoid collections? Be **PROACTIVE** and always communicate with your creditors. If you're having problems making payments, then tell them so they can help work out a payment plan that you can live with. Collections come when you haven't responded to the creditor and they sell your account to a collection company to pursue you for payment.

Protect your credit at all times. Your financial character matters and will help you reach the goals in your plan.

Chapter 11

What is Debt-To-Income Ratio (DTI) and how does it affect me?

The DTI is a major determining factor as to whether your mortgage application gets approved for a loan. You can have great credit with scores over 700 but if your debt-to-income ratio is too high the loan will not be approved.

Your debt-to-income ratio takes into account how much your monthly gross income is as compared to your total monthly debt obligations on your credit report and calculates a percentage. A rule of thumb is to keep your debt-to-income ratio under 50%, but even that's too high with some lenders. You really want to stay at 45% or less. Keep in mind, you are qualified on your gross income NOT your net, so that's before taxes and if your ratios are too high, you're not doing yourself any favors. It's putting you in harm's way of a potential foreclosure or bankruptcy.

Debt-to-income ratio is calculated by dividing your monthly minimum debt payments from your credit report plus your estimated mortgage payment by your monthly gross income (before taxes). Keep in mind, this doesn't include utilities, gas, and entertainment or childcare expenses.

Example 1: Your annual salary is $48,000 per year with a credit score of 680. You're seeking to qualify for a $150,000 mortgage with an estimated payment of $1150 per month. Your current debts on your credit report are $1250. We'll calculate what is called your front-end ratio, meaning how much of your income the mortgage payment alone represents and then your back-end ratio of what your total debt monthly represents of your gross income.

Monthly income is $48,000/12 = $4000 per month Gross

Estimated mortgage is $1150/4000 = **28.75% front end DTI ratio**

Total debt-to-income ratio is $1150 + $1250 =$2400/4000 = **60% back end DTI ratio which is too high for a loan approval.**

But let's say you did your homework and prepared for the mortgage and **paid off** an installment debt that was $650 per month before applying for a mortgage.

Example 2: Now we have the same monthly income $4000, estimated mortgage payment of $1150 but the credit report debt is only $600 not $1250. Now our ratios are different and more in line for approval.

Estimated mortgage is $1150/4000 = **28.75% front end DTI ratio**

Total debt-to-income ratio is $1150 + $600 =$1750/4000 = 43.75% back end DTI ratio which is great for a loan approval.

This is why it's so important to know where you are prior to applying for a mortgage so that you can put yourself in the best possible position to be approved and qualify for the home you want. Otherwise, you risk being declined because the ratios have been exceeded and don't meet the lender's guidelines.

TIP: If you want to take a short cut and know just how much of a mortgage payment you will qualify for, you can take your gross monthly income and multiply it by 45% as a rule of thumb and then subtract the minimum payment amounts on your credit report. So using the same numbers as in Example 2 above. $4000 monthly income x 45% = $1800 is the max amount of debt you can have. $1800 minus $600 debt on the credit report means your max mortgage payment is $1200.

Yes, it's possible to go higher than 45% DTI but ask yourself why you would want to. What borrowers forget to take into consideration is the increase in utilities when they purchase a home. Also remember that these ratios are before taxes so if you qualify on $4000 gross but you really net $3500 per month, ask if you are helping yourself or hurting yourself by exceeding the standard ratios of 45%.

Remember to live within your means and don't fall prey to buying the bigger house just because you like it. If the numbers run the risk of putting you into a financial challenge, then it's NOT worth it.

Chapter 12

How to clean up your credit report for Free

In America, you are entitled to a free credit report every twelve months.

By law, the FCRA, Fair Credit Reporting Act and the Fact Act protects the consumer's right to have an accurate credit report. If there is any erroneous information found on your credit report, you can dispute it. Each creditor has up to thirty days to respond to your dispute confirming the information is valid or **REMOVING** the information if it's not.

You can simply go online to request your free report from each agency – Equifax, TransUnion and Experian and review for accuracy through www.annualcreditreport.com or call them at 877-322-8228.

The reason why you need all three reports is because different creditors in different parts of the country report to specific agencies. Creditors are not required to report to all three agencies so you want to make sure you see everything. Example: in the state of Alaska, creditors report mainly to TransUnion, and in the state of Georgia, creditors report mainly to Equifax.

I suggest going online and signing up for a monitoring service so you know anytime something hits your credit from either agency. It'll help protect your credit and you can catch erroneous information quicker.

Mortgage lenders will pull a credit report called a Tri Merge so they can see all credit reported to all three agencies. You want to make sure you're seeing the same thing and that your report is correct to avoid any surprises.

Tip 1: When you dispute an account with any agency please make sure you follow up. You want to see a corrected report removing the item or, if the issue was validated, you want the verbiage to show **DISPUTE RESOLVED.** If you leave a dispute open, this will hurt you with a mortgage lender and may affect a loan approval.

Tip 2: Collection agencies have a tendency not to update your credit report when paid in full. Protect yourself by asking for a letter for any arrangements you made with a collection company and confirm they will update your credit report. If they fail to update your credit and you have to dispute the erroneous information, you have the letter.

You can contact the three agencies online, which is quicker, or you can print the form online a and mail to the appropriate address below:

TransUnion, LLC
P.O. Box 2000
Chester, PA 19016
800-916-8800
www.transunion.com

Equifax Information Svc, LLC
P.O. Box 740256
Atlanta, GA 30348
866-349-5191
www.equifax.com

Experian
P.O. Box 4500
Allen, TX 75013
888-397-3742
www.experian.com

Remember to review each item carefully to make sure it has been properly reported and updated and, if not, open a claim and dispute those items for free and submit any paperwork to prove your claim. This is the same thing people try to charge you for to have them clean up your credit.

Chapter 13

Celebrating Milestones and Achieving Success

You're almost there. It's important to celebrate the milestones. It keeps you thinking positive and focused on your goals and plan.

The next step is to go back to your plan outline and add timeframes/actual date deadlines to it. But you must know your discharge date before you can tweak your plan with actual date deadlines for opening new accounts, etc.

I'm a visual person and I believe in vision boards. I keep one on the wall next to my bed so it's the first thing I see when I wake up. I mark off my accomplishments as I reach them. You may want to try this for yourself to help you stay focused.

Learning the lessons:

Now you're in the state of mind to look back over your life's journey and see the lessons you needed to learn. Be real and honest with yourself. It's never too late to change habits and put yourself in a better position to be successful. But we must learn and grow from our mistakes, so we don't repeat them.

Keep your eyes on the prize and rebuild your life. Plan how you want to live and work your plan. **Success is what you make it, so don't limit yourself.** Good luck.

It's been my sincere hope to bring value to you. I hope this book has helped open your eyes as to how you can succeed after bankruptcy. My wish for you is that you recover from bankruptcy stronger and better than ever in a short amount of time.

Chapter 13

Thank you for allowing me to share my life's journey with you.

Thanks for reading. I hope you found this book useful. I welcome all honest feedback positive or negative. If you would be so kind as to leave a review on the website where you got the book.

www.ingramcontent.com/pod-product-compliance
Lightning Source LLC
Chambersburg PA
CBHW070756050426
42452CB00010B/1864